A

CATALOGUE

OF THE
GENUINE and VALUABLE
COLLECTION
OF
COINS and MEDALS,

Of that ingenious and well-known Collector

Mr. *Nathaniel Samm,*
Of *Bartholomew Cloſe,*
𝕷𝖆𝖙𝖊𝖑𝖞 𝕯𝖊𝖈𝖊𝖆𝖘'𝖉;

Which (by ORDER of the ADMINISTRATRIX)

Will be ſold by AUCTION,

By Mr. LANGFORD and Son,

At their Houſe in the *Great Piazza, Covent
Garden,*

On *Wedneſday* the 3d, and *Thurſday* the 4th of
this Inſtant *Auguſt* 1768.

The ſame may be viewed on *Monday* the Firſt of *Auguſt,*
and every Day after from *Ten* till *Four,* and the Sale
will begin each Day punctually at *Twelve o'Clock.*

Catalogues may be had *gratis* on the Days of Viewing,
at Mr. LANGFORD's aforeſaid.

English *Copper Medals.*

18 A fine medal of the Czar Peter, struck at Paris, and one by Daſſier ——— ———
19 Three of Chriſtina Queen of *Sweden*, 1 of them gilt
20 King of Poland, Duke of Lorrain, Prince of Orange, Prince Ferdinand, and 3 more ———
21 Phillip V. King of Spain, Dutcheſs of Orleans, Caſſini, Duke Radzivil, and Abb. Forniſarius
22 Martin Luther 2, Card Coſtaguta, Dutcheſs of Arſchot, and 2 more ——— ———
23 Dukes of Parma, Mantua, Florence, and Livius Odeſchalchi Duke of Bracciano ———
24 Three of Lewis XIV, one of the Princeſs of Condé, and 2 more ——— ———

Popes Medals.

25 THirty-two of different Popes ———
26 A compleat ſet from Martin V. to Benedict XIV. incluſive, 1 of each, *in 4 boards* ———
27 Another the ſame, *in 4 boards* ———
28 Martin V. 1—Eugenius IV. 1—Sixtus IV. 1—Innocent VIII. 1—Sixtus V. 2—Urban VIII. 7—Gregory XIII. 1—Innocent X. 1—Alexander VII. 5—Clement IX. 2—Clement X. 3—Clement XI. 11— Innocent XI. 4—Clement XII. 1—Benedict XIII. 1—Innocent XII. 2 ———
29 Nicholas V, Eugenius IV, Pius III, Urban VIII. 6 —Gregory XIII, Clement IX. 5—Clement X. 5 —Alexander VII. 7—Innocent XI. 4— Clement XI. 4—Innocent XII. 2—Clement XII. 1—Benedict XIII. 2 ——— ———
30 Julius III, Gregory XIII. 2—Paul V, Urban VIII. 14—Innocent X. 5—Innocent XI. 7—Alexander VIII. 1—Benedict XIII. Benedict XIV.
31 Pius IV. 2—Paul V. 1—Clement VIII. 1—Sixtus V. 1—Gregory XIII. 1—Urban VIII. 2—Clement X. 1—Alexander VIII. 1—Innocent XI. 3—Innocent XII. 4—Clement XI. 4—Clement XII. 4—Benedict XIII. 2—Innocent XIII. 1
32 Sixtus IV, Alexander VI, Julius II. 2—Julius III. 1—Paul III. 2—Gregory XIII. 1—Paul V. 2—Sixtus V. 1—Urban VIII. 2—Innocent IX. 1—Alexander VII. 4—Clement IX. 1—Clement X.

3—Innocent XI. 3—Clement XI. 3—Innocent
XIII. 1—Benedict XIII. 1 ——————
33 Eugenius IV, Paul V. 1—Sixtus V. 3—Urban VIII.
2—Alexander VII. 4—Innocent XI. 4—Clement
XI. 12—Innocent XII. 1 ——————

Silver Coins and Medals.

34 FOreign coins of moſt nations, wt. 15 oz. 19 dwts.
35 Ditto, wt. 15 oz. 15 dwts.
36 Ten roman catholick ſaints, &c. with loops, ſeveral
by Hameranus, wt. 2 oz. 18 dwts. 12 gr.
37 Ditto, wt. 2 oz. 18 dwts. 12 gr.
38 Ditto, wt. 1 oz. 19 dwts. 12 gr.
39 A fine medal of the two De Witts, 1 of the preſent
Prince of Orange, 1 of the King of Pruſſia, and
1 more, wt. 4 oz. 19 dwts. 12 gr.
40 Four medals of Lewis XIV, and 4 of Lewis XV, wt.
4 oz. 16 dwts.
41 Card. Fleury by Rotier, 2 of Lewis XV, and 4 more,
wt. 7 oz. 16 dwts.
42 Queen of Hungary, Emperor Joſeph, a Venetian
medal of Jo. Cornelii, and 5 more, wt. 4 oz. 18
dwts. 12 gr.
43 Francis I. Emperor, and 9 other miſcellaneous medals,
wt. 5 oz. 11 dwts 12 gr.
44 Prince Eugene, John of Leyden, Alphonſus VI, and
12 more different, wt. 5 oz. 18 dwts. 12 gr.
45 Frederick IV, Sop. Magdalena Queen of Denmark,
and 5 more Daniſh medals, wt 5 oz. 13 dwts.
46 Two medals of Card. Mazarine, and 1 of Cardinal
Richlieu, wt. 2 oz. 4 dwts.
47 Three fine medals of Chriſtina Queen of Sweden, wt.
1 oz. 16 dwts.
48 One of Mich. Molinos, 1 of John Scheyfue, and 1 of
Zuichem, wt. 4 oz. 9 dwts. 12 gr.

Engliſh Silver Coins.

49 ENgliſh coins of ſeveral Princes, wt. 4 oz. 12 dwts.
50 Henry III. *Rex Ang.* and 16 more half groats,
pence and half pence
51 James I. crown gilt, a commonwealth half crown
1649, an Oliver's ſhilling, a Baltimore ſixpence,
and 2 fine ditto of Elizabeth
52 Seven ſhillings, 5 ſixpences, 5 groats, and 10 more
Engliſh of ſeveral reigns

53 A

53 A penny of Alexander II, a groat of James III, a crown of Mary, and 7 more Scotch coins — 11 — 12

54 Oliver Cromwell's crown, half crown and shilling, *in the highest preservation* — 3 5 " 5

55 Mary Queen of Scots, with her head, *fine* — 1 2 " 6

56 Elizabeth's mill'd sixpence 1574, *very rare*, and a fine mill'd twopence of ditto — 2 2 " 8 "

57 A fine mill'd six-pence of Charles I, and 2 fine half groats of ditto. by Briot — 3 2 " 7 "

58 Anlaf, a rare unpublished penny — 1 1 " 2 "

English Silver Medals.

59 A Fine medal of Queen Elizabeth, rev. Noah's Ark, *Sevas Tranquilla Per Undas, very rare* — 6 " 6 "

60 A jetton of ditto *Quid Nos*, 2 different ones of Prince Henry, and 1 of Lord Buckhurst — 4 3 " 11 "

61 Six medals and jettons of Charles I. and his Queen — 6 1 " 1 "

62 Charles I. Scotch coronation medal, Charles II. ditto at Scoon, and another by Simons — 3 0 " 10 "

63 A rare medal of Fairfax, and another George Duke of Albemarle — 2 1 " 16 —

64 Charles II. 3 different medals, and 1 on Charles XI. receiving the order of the garter, wt. 6 oz. — 2 " 7 —

65 Charles II. and Queen Catherine 3 different, 1 on the Restoratio , Dutchess of Portsmouth, and one of James II. — 6. 2 " 15

66 Charles II. *Magna Opera Domini*, by Simon, *fine* — 1 1 " 15

67 Charles II. *Felicitas Britannia*, wt. 6 oz. 18 dwts. — 4 " 5

68 Charles II. *Nullum Numen Abest*, wt. 3 oz. 8 dwts. — 1 " 16

69 A fine medal of the Duke of Lauderdale, by Rotier, wt. 3 oz. 3 dwts. — 1 " 16

70 Ditto of Archbishop Laud, by *ditto*

71 Ditto of the Earl of Shaftesbury, Dr. Sacheverell, and on the peace of Breda — 1 " 13

72 James II. on the beheading of Argyle and Monmouth — 1 " 8

73 James II. on the birth of the Chevalier — 1 " 17
— 3 " 3

Foreign Gold.

74 TWenty-one ducats, pistoles, &c. of France, Holland, Germany, Sweden, &c. wt. 2 oz. 5 dwts. 16 gr. — 9 " 5

75 Twenty-nine ditto, wt. 1 oz. 18 dwts. 21 gr. — 7 " 17

76 A fine bust of Queen Dido, 2 small medals of Gustavus Adolphus, 1 of Frederick and Louisa King

and

62 . 2

and Queen of Denmark, and 1 more, wt. 6 dwts. 5 gr.   1 „ 13 „ 0

77 Christina Queen of Sweden, a fine medal, wt. 18 dwts.   3 - 17 „ 0

78 Leonora wife to the Emperor Frederick, wt. 15 dwts. 17 gr.   3 - 1 „ —

79 Medals, coins, casts, &c.   37 — 7 —

80 A silver medal of Clement XII. in a frame, 4 copper Popes ditto, 1 gilt, and 2 more   1 „ 8 —

81 An halfpenny of George, the head, letters, and figures in gold   1 „ 6 —

82 A neat japan medal cabinet   2 „ 2 —

    13 „ 8 „ 6

Second Day's Sale, *Thursday, August* 4.

English Copper Medals.

Lot

1 Charles Ist, Queen Mary 2, Anne 1, George II. Prince Frederick Duke of Cumberland, and George IIId.   8 0 „ 16 „ 6

2 George IId and the Royal Family, a fine medal   0 „ 18 „ 0

3 Two gilt medals of Charles IId and Queen Mary, two of Oliver Cromwell, Sir Isaac Newton, and one of the Chevalier   6 2 „ 18 „ 6

4 George 1, Prince Frederick, Dr. Freind, Mr. Folkes, and 2 more   6 1 „ 14 „ 0

5 Sir Francis Bacon, Duke of Marlborough, Dr. Barker, and Archbishop Wake   4 1 „ 2 „ 0

6 The Chevalier *Unica Salus,* and Princess Clementina *Fortunam Causamque Sequor, fine*   2 1 „ 9 —

7 Ditto with both their heads, and 2 fine ones with those of their two sons both different, *fine*   3 2 „ 6 —

8 Ditto *Cujus Est,* and the young Chevalier *Amor Et Spes*   2 0 „ 17 „ 6

9 Martin Folkes, Esq; *very fine*   1 — 12 —

10 Sir John Barnard, Card. Fleury, King of Spain and Queen of Hungary, by Dassier, *fine*   4 7 „ 2 —

11 A fine bust of *Pompeius Magnus,* by Warin, and one ditto of Henry the IVth   2 0 „ 5 —

12 Card. Norris, Portocarrero, Azzolino, Maximus, Gozzadini, Marshal Turenne, and 4 more   10 2 „ 8 —

13 Lewis XIII. and Cardinal Fleury, 2 fine medals with the same rev. by Warin   2 0 „ 10 „ 6

14 Cardinal Fleury, as the last, *but extremely fine*   4 „ 2 „ 0

15 Marshal Count Saxe, in gold and copper, *fine*   4 „ 7 „ 0

16 Julius

    17 „ 1 „ 0

Popes Medals.

16 Julius III. 2—Paul III. 3—Paul IV. 1—Pius IV. 3
— Clement VI, Paul V. 2 — Urban VIII. 2 —
Clement X. 2—Innocent XI. 2 — Clement XI. 5
—Innocent XII. 1 — Clement XII. 1 —Innocent
—Benedict XIII. 3   29

17 ... ...—Paul IV. 1—Paul V. 2—Sixtus V. 1—
Clement VIII 2—Gregory XIII. 3—Urban VIII.
1—Innocent X. 3—Alexander VII. 2 — Clement
IX. 1—Clement X. 2 — Innocent XII, Clement
XI. 5—Clement XII. 2—Benedict XIII. 2   28

18 Adrian VI, Clement VI, Clement IX. 4—Clement
X. 3—Alexander VII. 5—Alexander VIII. 1—
Innocent XI. 3 — Clement XI. 3 — Innocent XII.
3—Clement XII. 3—Innocent XIII. 2—Benedict
XIII. 3   31

19 Innocent X, Clement X 3—Clement XI. 7 — Innocent XII. 3 — Benedict XIII, Innocent XIII, Card
Coleia, Card. Nerlius, Odeschalchi, and the Card.
of Hesse   20

20 Paul III. 1—Alexander VIII. 1 — Clement IX, and
Innocent XII.   4

21 Innocent XII. 2 very fine and gilt, 1 by *Beatrix Hame-
rani*   2

22 A fine damask'd medal of Clement XII, by Daffier   1

23 A fine set of the Dukes of Lorrain, by St. Urbain, *very
rare*   37

Roman *Silver.*

24 Accoleia, Egnatia, Hirtia, Cloulia, Lucilia, Mi-
nucia, Hos. Sentia, and 26 other different
families   35

25 Gellia, Harucella, Procilia, Norbana, Tullia, and·
29 other families   35

26 The twelve Cæsars   12

27 Lucilian, Antoninus, Aurelius, Verus, Commodus,
Sept. Severus, Caracalla, Elagabalus, with their
wives, Sabina, Faustina, Lucilla, Crispina, Julia
Pia, Plautilla, and Julia Paula   16

28 Different Emperors and Empresses, *some scarce reverses*   48

29 Gordianus 17, Phillipus 9, Otascilla   28

30 Traj. Decius 6, Etruscilla 3, Herennius 2, Hostilian
1, Treb. Gallus 3, Volusian 2   17

31 Æmi.

Æmilian 1, Valerian 5, Mariniana 1, Gallienus 7, La-
lonina 3, Valerian, jun. 2 —————— 19 — 5 „ 6
32 Alex. Severus 7, Jul. Mammea 2, Saluſtia Barbia 1,
Maximinus 2 —————— — 12 — 3 „ 6

Pope's Medals, in Silver.

33 CLement X, Innocent XI, Clement XI, Innocent XII,
and 3 more, wt. 6 oz. 1 dwt. —————— 1 „ 18 „ —
34 Innocent X, Innocent XI, Clement XI, Innocent XII,
and Benedict XIII, wt. 4 oz. 18 dwts. 12 gr. —— 1 „ 12 —
35 Julius II, Gregory XIII, Pius V, Urban VIII, Gregory XV, Clement XI, wt. 4 oz. 6 dwts. —— 1 „ 6 —
36 Clement X, Innocent X, Innocent XI, Innocent XII.
wt. 4 oz. 3 dwts. 12 gr. —————— 1 „ 5 —
37 Alexander VIII, Innocent XII, Clement XI, Clement
XII, Benedict XIII, wt. 4 oz. 2 dwts. 12 gr. —— 1 „ 5 —
38 Innocent XI, Alexander VIII, Benedict XIII, Benedict XIV, wt. 4 oz. — 1 „ 5 —
39 Clement XII, Benedict XIII, Benedict XIV, wt. 4 oz.
7 dwts. — 1 „ 11 „ 6
40 Julius II, Urban VIII, Innocent XI, Clement XI,
Innocent XIII. Benedict XIII, wt. 4 oz. —— 1 „ 7 —
41 Urban VIII, Innocent IX, Clement XII, Innocent
XIII, Benedict XIII, and 1 more, wt. 3 oz. 16 dwts.
12 gr. —————— 1 „ 3 —
42 A fine buſt of Clement XI, wt. 3 oz. —————— „ 17 „ 6
43 Clement XII, rev. *Adorate Dominum in Atrio Sancto
Ejus*, wt. 5 oz. 7 dwts. 12 gr. —————— 2 „ 11 —
44 Ditto, rev. *Sacello In Lateranen Baſil St. Andrea Corſinio
Aedificatio*, wt. 5 oz. 8 dwts. 2 „ 13 —

Engliſh Gold.

45 THREE rude ancient britiſh coins, wt. 9 dwts. 12 gr. — 1 „ 6 —
46 Edward III. a noble, a ſpur ryal, and a thirty
ſhilling piece of James I. wt. 17 dwts. 9 gr. 3—3 „ 11 —
47 Henry VI. a ſalute, *rare* —————— 1 — 1 „ 5 —
48 Henry VIII. a pound ſovereign, an half ſovereign, a
crown нк, and an half ſovereign of Edward VI,
wt. 17 dwts. 14 gr. —————— 4 3 „ 12 —
49 An half ſovereign, and 2 half quarters hammer'd, and
2 mill'd half ſovereigns, wt. 13 dwts. —— 2 „ 10 —
50 Elizabeth, a mill'd half, and 1 qr. ſovereign 2 — 1 „ 18 —
51 Elizabeth, a fine ſpur ryal, *very rare* —————— 1 — 4 „ 0 „ 0
52 James I. an half, 1qr. 1-fifth, and 1-eighth ſovereign
B   a

37 „ 5 „ 0

a sovereign, and an half ditto of Charles I, wt. 15 dwts. 18 gr.

53 James I. a fine pattern piece, and a small medal of Charles I. with a rose and feathers ————

54 Oliver Cromwell his half broad, *finely preferv'd, very rare* ————

55 Oliver Cromwell his fine medal, *Non Deficient Oliva*

56 Charles I. an angel, an unite, half unite of Charles II, and 2 others, wt. 15 dwts. 12 gr. ————

57 Charles II. medal, or pattern, *Magnalia Dei, in the highest preservation* ———— ————

58 Charles I. the coronation medal at Skoon, wt. 7 dwts. 22 gr. ————

59 James II. a touch piece, and a fine one of the Chevalier

60 Anne, a fine pattern guinea AR, and a proof with the rose ———— ————

61 George I. a fine guinea *Pr. Ele,* and a proof double guinea of George II,

62 Mary Queen of Scots, 2 fine pieces with her head

63 James II. an unicorn and lyon, and 2 pieces of Charles I, wt. 8 dwts. 11 gr.

64 James V. 2 pieces with the head, and one of Mary, no head ———— ————

English Silver Medals.

65 JAMES II. and his Queen, 2 ditto and the Chevalier, and a fine rare one on the birth of the Chevalier

66 William III. 3 different medals, 1 of them gilt, wt. 3 oz. 19 dwts. ————

67 Anne, a fine medal, Nova Palladium Troja, wt. 3 oz. 10 dwts. ————

68 Anne ditto, on giving up the Tenths ————

69 Anne ditto on the taking of Lisle, Barcelona, &c. wt. 3 oz. 14 dwts. 12 gr. ————

70 Anne, a farthing, *Pax Missa Per Orbem,* 1 with the portico, and 1 more, *in fine preservation*

71 George I 2 on the battle of Preston and sea fight off Sicily, and two of George II. on his marriage, and the taking of Pondicherry, wt. 3 oz. 15 dwts. ————

72 George III. and Queen Charlotte their coronation medals, and 1 with their heads on each side, *fine*

73 Prince Frederick, by Koch, *finely preserv'd* ————

74 Duke of Cumberland, by Yeo and Pingo ————

75 Eight coronation medals of Charles II, James II, William and Mary, Anne, George I. and George II, wt. 4 oz. 3 dwts. 12 gr.

76 Twe

76 Two busts of the Chevalier and his sister, a fine medal of Princess Clementina, and 1 more ——— 3 1 „ 12 „ 0

77 The Chevaliers medal, *Cujus Est Reddite,* 3 jettons, 2 angels, and 1 other piece of ditto ——— 7 1 „ 3 —

78 Ditto *Unica Salus,* and 1 of Princess Clementina, *Fortunam Causamque Sequor, finely preserv'd,* in a velvet case, mounted in silver ——— 2 2 „ 6 —

79 Ditto with both their heads, on their marriage, and the birth of their eldest son ——— ——— 2 2 „ 2 —

80 The young Chevalier and his brother, *fine* ——— 1 1 „ 4 „ 6

81 Another ditto, different, *gilt* ——— 1 — 16 „ 6

82 Another fine, *Amor Et Spes* ——— 1 „ 3 —

83 Another fine, *Riverescit* ——— 1 „ 6 —

84 Two enamell'd crowns of Queen Anne, and a bust of ditto ——— 1 „ 2 —

85 A porter's ticket, and 13 other jettons, half-pence, &c. wt. 3 oz. 7 dwts. 12 gr. ——— 1 „ 2 —

86 A medal of the King of Poland, a fine mill'd shilling of Elizabeth, and a gilt medal of Lewis XI. and Anne of Britany ——— 2 „ 6 —

87 A screw dollar of Gustavus Adolphus, and 11 others — 1 „ 3 —

88 Fifty-five counters of the Kings of England, &c. in a box, by the oz. ——— 2 „ 2 —

89 Oliver Cromwell, George I, Sir Isaac Newton, and 1 more ——— 1 „ 0 „ 0

90 A fine bust inscribed, *Nec Elatus. Nec Dejectus* ——— 0 „ 13 „ 2

91 Billon coins of several nations ——— 18 — 4 „ 6

92 A fine set of the reformers, by Dassier, with the medal of Archbishop Wake, to whom they were dedicated, in a neat shagreen case ——— 25 4 „ 10 „ 0

93 A small mahogany medal cabinet ——— 18 „ 6

26 „ 13 „ 6

F I N I S.